Managing Dyspepsia

A SELF-HELP FOODIES GUIDE

JENNIFER JACKSON

MANAGING DYSPEPSIA: A SELF-HELP FOODIES GUIDE

Natural approaches to help you manage functional dyspepsia and boost your digestive health. Includes advice, meal plans and delicious gut-friendly recipes.

DISCLAIMER

The information featured in this book is based on the author's personal experiences, research and learnings. It mentions health practitioners who have helped the author manage dyspepsia but is not intended as a substitute for medical advice.

This book does not contain all information available on the subject, and other sources of information about dyspepsia are available.

Every effort has been made to make this book as accurate as possible. However, there may be typographical and / or content errors. Therefore, this book should serve only as a general guide and not as the ultimate source of subject information.

The author and any persons or organisations mentioned in the book shall have no liability or responsibility to any person or entity regarding any loss or damage incurred, or alleged to have incurred, directly or indirectly, by the information contained in this book.

Contents

My dyspepsia story 3

What is dyspepsia? 5

What causes dyspepsia? 6

How to heal your gut naturally 8

Alternative therapies 13

Foods to add, avoid and reduce 17

The benefits of steam cooking 19

Sample dyspepsia meal plan 20

Gut-friendly recipes 22

Scrumptious starters & light bites 24

    Lemony Steamed Asparagus 25

    Steamed Aromatic Cumin Cauliflower........................ 26

    Avocado & Olive Bruschetta 27

    Mentally Good Lentil Soup 28

    Poached Egg on Sourdough with Avocado................. 29

    Baked Aubergine with Yoghurt Dressing 30

    Cooling Tappouli 31

Marvellous mains 33

    Soothing Chicken & Vegetable Broth 34

    Steamed Chicken, Carrot & Courgette 35

    Moroccan Spiced Sweet Potato & Bone Broth Stew 36

    Cabbage & Lamb Stew.. 37

    Pretty in Pink Salmon 'n' Slaw.................................... 38

    Homely Dolma 39

    Mama's Veggie Biryani... 40

Bone Broth Bolognese 41

Delectable desserts 43

Warm Blueberry & Coconut Muffins 44

Kefir Yoghurt with Manuka Honey..............................45

Cinnamon Peaches...46

Rose Water Beetroot Brownies....................................47

Delicious drinks...48

Checklist to avoid dyspepsia...52

My dyspepsia story

As a 'foodie', I enjoy cooking and eating a variety of international cuisine, so I was in for a bit of a shock in January 2013 when I discovered I had developed 'Functional Dyspepsia' - that is, dyspepsia with no underlying disease. To keep the flare-ups at bay, I felt that bland soup was pretty much my only safe meal choice. Luckily it wasn't forever and I can now even eat chocolate and cakes in moderation. Ultimately, food probably wasn't the root cause but it certainly plays a major role in managing the symptoms.

What happened?

Two weeks after the birth of my first daughter by emergency Caesarean, I started experiencing intense stomach pains that would rise to my chest like heartburn, to the point where it felt like a mild heart attack. It first happened while walking to the doctor's surgery. By the time I arrived, I was cowering towards the floor. The doctor gave me oxygen, checked my pulse and blood pressure, then got me blue-lighted to hospital where they kept me in for tests. This included a CT scan to check for pulmonary embolism (a potentially fatal lung clot). To my relief and frustration, all tests came back negative and I was sent home with no diagnosis after three days.

However, my symptoms kept recurring and I recall feeling like a failure for having to hand the baby to my husband, just as breastfeeding was becoming established. I also felt anxious that a serious illness was ensuing. At my follow-up, the doctor suggested I may have developed 'severe dyspepsia', so he prescribed me some omeprazole, a proton pump inhibitor (PPI), to reduce my stomach acidity. He advised me to avoid spicy food, alcohol and any other foods that triggered the dyspepsia 'attack'. These turned out to include pastries (especially mince pies, which is what I had eaten just before heading to the doctors' that time, as we were celebrating Christmas a few weeks late), chocolate and fried foods, as well as juices, hot chocolate and coffee.

Taking control of my health

After complying with the doctor's advice and persevering with the omeprazole for a few months (it did help somewhat), I decided to conduct my own research, mainly online to begin with. I learned that the regular doses of painkillers, diclofenac and nurofen, which I was given following the C-section, had most likely affected my stomach. I wasn't used to taking so many painkillers. This, along with the stress I had experienced with the understaffed hospital chaos during labour, abdominal scarring from the caesarean, and the worry around my newborn having a life threatening 'suspected sepsis' with 10 days in intensive care, may have caused, or at least triggered, my digestive imbalance.

Six years later, a specialist midwife retrospectively diagnosed me with mild post-traumatic stress. I later also discovered that long term use of PPIs can actually make you more ill because they reduce your stomach acid which is in fact essential for optimal digestion. I felt compelled to seek alternative natural remedies and advice. And that's when I started to understand the importance of healing the gut for overall health.

I'm pleased to report, touch wood, that when I had my second child recently I was able to keep dyspepsia at bay. It hasn't completely vanished as I still have to be careful not to pig out on too much chocolate, cheese, alcohol and fried foods, but at least I can enjoy these in moderation.

Learning to manage dyspepsia

With the help of Advanced Clinical & Sports Massage Therapist, Albert Dutoit, along with the information I'd found out through my own research, I soon learned to manage my dyspepsia episodes with stretches, relaxation and diet, which was empowering. On the rare occasions (about once a year) where it becomes persistent over a number of days or weeks and I struggle to manage it myself, I might book an appointment with Albert. I've since learned that acupuncture could help too. More on these treatments later in the section on 'Alternative therapies'.

This self-help guide is based on my own personal experiences and online research, as well as advice from amazing natural therapists who have helped me along the way. I hope it will help you manage your dyspepsia naturally, heal your gut and allow you to enjoy food at the same time.

What is dyspepsia?

Before we delve into the causes of dyspepsia, let's explain what exactly we mean by the term:

'Dyspepsia (indigestion) is a term which describes pain and sometimes other symptoms which come from your upper gut (the stomach, oesophagus or duodenum).' Symptoms may include pain or discomfort in your upper tummy, acid reflux, bloating, belching, quickly feeling full after eating, nausea and vomiting.'

PATIENT.INFO

Functional dyspepsia, also known as non-ulcer dyspepsia, is the term given to chronic indigestion that does not have an obvious cause. After ruling out serious underlying causes, this was my diagnosis. It was a relief but also frustrating.

While most people experience odd bouts of functional dyspepsia, such as after a spicy meal, it can affect your long term quality of life even if it's not very serious. For example, during the first few months after my first dyspepsia attack, I had frequent, albeit less dramatic episodes, which made me reticent about taking my baby out in the car on my own in case I got caught out while driving. My husband was reluctant to go anywhere and leave me on my own apart from to go to work. The world of dyspepsia was new and scary to me and I didn't know how to manage it at the time.

I've since become aware that many of my friends and relatives are experiencing acid reflux and similar dyspepsia episodes. I recently joined a few Facebook groups where I was shocked to see hundreds of other people experiencing a whole host of digestive issues. It certainly appears that dyspepsia is on the rise.

What causes dyspepsia?

There are many reasons why we are seeing more digestive and gut disorders and diseases. Here are some of the main causes:

"Eating too much processed, dead and devitalised food that is devoid of enzymes, eating too much, too late, too quickly, medications, environmental toxins, and prolonged excessive stress, all affect the delicate balance of enzymes and bacteria needed to maintain a healthy digestive system and gut."

LINDA BOOTH, NATUROPATH AND FOUNDER, JUST FOR TUMMIES

Low stomach acid

One cause of dyspepsia for some people is a lack of acid in the stomach. This problem increases with age, stress, certain medications, and vitamin deficiencies such as zinc and vitamin B (caused by inadequate dietary intake or by nutrient loss through stress, smoking or alcohol consumption).

When you eat, the acid in your stomach tells the sphincter in your oesophagus to close. If there is not enough acid, the oesophagus may not close and pushes the food up your throat, which is what causes the acid reflux or pain. That's why certain foods can't then be tolerated very well.

Silent reflux

Silent reflux is like acid reflux except you may not realise it happening until some damage has been caused by the stomach acid. It can be triggered by pregnancy, a physical deformity in the oesophagus or lifestyle factors such as poor diet. It may present to you as a tickly cough, sore throat, hoarse voice or post nasal drip instead. In some cases a runny nose (post-nasal drip) can be caused by silent reflux.

Hiatus hernia

It is common to suffer with dyspepsia and acid reflux when someone has a hiatus hernia. In Naturopath Linda Booth's experience, many hiatus hernias are caused by bloated, expanded and stretched intestines.

"If the bloating can be reduced, the hiatus hernia can be reduced and thus no need for the PPI", she explains. Bloated, gassy intestines can push up into the stomach and through the diaphragm, pushing acid-drenched food out of the stomach and up the oesophagus.

"Excess weight around the midriff can also cause a hiatus hernia so weight management is key", adds Linda. "I always recommend taking one of our Live Bacteria capsules before breakfast and before bed with a small glass of water, one of our natural Digestive Enzyme tablets just before lunch and one just before dinner, and if you are not eating oily fish at least three times weekly, one of our Omega 3 capsules daily with food. Initially I ask for a commitment of 30 days to this protocol, then contact me or one of my team after this time to discuss symptoms."

Abdominal scarring

In my case, my caesarean caused abdominal scarring which may have played a major role in causing dyspepsia, along with pregnancy itself. As my external scar had healed well on the outside, I had no idea how awful the internal scarring still was seven years later until I had my second child by caesarean and the surgeon described it to me. More on this in the section on alternative therapies.

How to heal your gut naturally

Digestive health is a key factor for maintaining a strong immune system. If your gut is inflamed it can wreak havoc with your health.

"Our digestive health has a lot to do with our immune health and vice versa. Its role in maintaining our immune health and, eventually, our overall wellbeing, cannot be underestimated. The two systems work closely to keep us in good physical and mental shape. With around 70-80% of the body's immune cells located in the gut, to have a healthy and resilient immune system requires a healthy gut."

LINDA BOOTH, NATUROPATH AND FOUNDER, JUST FOR TUMMIES

Feed your gut

Feeding your gut, whether you have dyspepsia or not, is key to overall health. One of the best sources of gut-friendly nutrition I have come across is bone broth. It can be laborious and extremely time consuming to make it yourself properly from scratch, and the only supermarket I can see selling good quality bone broths is Ocado.

However, during the pandemic lockdown in March and April 2020 I was struggling to get online delivery slots, so I decided to look for direct suppliers. That's when I came across a company called Boil & Broth in Dorset and have since got in touch with Rachel Down, the company's founder, for her insights.

"Nutrition is the key to long term health. The gut is where digestion happens, so having a balanced diet of all natural foods means that your gut will function at its optimum level, resulting in your body being enriched with the nutrients and minerals it needs to function."

RACHEL DOWN, FOUNDER, BOIL & BROTH

Rachel is also a BSc health science student and insists that gut health plays a key role in preventing, managing and curing dyspepsia: "Having good gut health, with a particular focus on your gut flora, can help reduce the symptoms of dyspepsia. The condition is usually linked to lifestyle factors such as eating too much of certain food types, eating too quickly, and stress."

To improve your gut health you should consider the foods you are already eating, says Rachel, who offers the following tips:

Cut back on carbs: Most people eat too many carbohydrates, so cutting back on bread, pizza, pasta, biscuits, cakes and other starchy sugary foods is a really great place to start.

Top up on veggies, protein and HDL fats: Replace some of the carbs with a diet rich in vegetables and high protein, including broths, meat, and eggs, and HDL fats such as fatty fish, olives, nuts, coconut foods and avocados.

Include more legumes and grains: Try quinoa, buckwheat and bulgur wheat.

Reduce inflammation: Gut inflammation is one of the major causes of digestive problems, so taking an approach to reducing inflammation is an important one.

Drink bone broth: In natural medicine, bone broth is believed to help reduce inflammation of the gut because of the natural proteins within broth itself.

Regulate your stomach acid levels

You can bring your stomach acid levels back to a healthy level by:

- Avoiding caffeine, alcohol and processed food.
- Reducing stress.
- Exercising more.
- Not drinking a lot of fluids during or right before a meal.
- Chewing food properly (to a paste).
- Eating probiotic-rich fermented foods, available in supermarkets, such as:
  - Kimchi
  - Sauerkraut
  - Kefir
  - kombucha
- Regularly drinking bone broths such as those by Boil & Broth.
- Taking probiotic supplements such as Just for Tummies' Live Bacteria and Digestive Enzymes or Holland & Barrett's Acidophilus.

Avoid medication where possible

Unfortunately, many people are reliant on Proton Pump Inhibitor medicines (PPIs), which can create a vicious circle and make the problem worse long term.

"Proton Pump Inhibitors are strong antacids that dramatically reduce the production of stomach acid. Regular, long-term use can allow pathogens into the digestive system via the oral route that would normally be 'nuked' by stomach acid. Lack of sufficient stomach acid can lead to improper digestion of food and weakened digestion, with the absorption of certain nutrients being blocked."

LINDA BOOTH, NATUROPATH AND FOUNDER, JUST FOR TUMMIES

"It has been documented that regular, long-term use of PPIs can increase the risk of gut infections like C. difficile", warns Linda. "However, it does need to be borne in mind that with diseases like Barrett's Oesopaghus, a precursor to oesophageal cancer, regurgitation of acid-drenched food out of the stomach and into the oesophagus has to be avoided, hence the need for PPIs in such cases.

"With the help of your GP and a naturopath or nutritional therapist it is possible to be weaned off PPIs, using diet, lifestyle and supplement protocols, in particular live bacteria and natural digestive enzymes."

Linda emphasises that first and foremost, for anyone who suffers with indigestion, dyspepsia, heartburn or acid reflux, it is important to get a proper diagnosis from your GP to rule out anything sinister.

I had an endoscopy a few years ago after experiencing severe symptoms again. It did not detect any abnormalities. I found the endoscopy procedure itself to be extremely unpleasant so if you need one, you may want to opt for full sedation so that you don't feel the camera going down your throat.

Linda concludes: "If there is no sinister reason for your symptoms, I would ask you to make some simple and immediate changes to how and when you eat. The last meal of the day should be the smallest one. Chew each mouthful for at least

30 seconds, until the food is like a paste, before swallowing. Don't drink water with meals and don't eat when you're feeling stressed, emotional or angry."

Alternative therapies

Remedial massage

When dyspepsia first struck, the main treatment that began to alleviate my symptoms was remedial massage and some very useful advice from Albert Dutoit, an Advanced Clinical and Sports Massage Therapist.

Albert helped me understand the problem and reassured me it was probably nothing too serious. He gave me the tools, such as exercise techniques, to address the triggers as they happen, and he also empowered me to deal with the discomfort in a positive way.

> *"Remedial massage can be very helpful to people suffering from dyspepsia. It works by unblocking any restrictions in the abdominal area through massage and reducing the tightness that forms around the diaphragm, which could have been triggered by stress and breathing dysfunctions."*
>
> ALBERT DUTOIT, ADVANCED CLINICAL AND SPORTS MASSAGE THERAPIST

In his clinic, Albert has found that most women who suffer from dyspepsia have either had a caesarean or other abdominal surgery.

"The resulting scar formation is quite often the cause or trigger for dyspepsia", he explains. "Scar adhesions often contribute to the restrictions developing around the diaphragm and also affect the overall digestive system. Furthermore, postnatal weakness in the core muscles can add to this, compounding the issue further.

"Using a combination of myofascial massage and targeted stretching techniques to relax and create space around the abdominal area can greatly reduce the intensity of the condition."

As a rule of thumb, Albert advises to focus on lengthening the front and strengthening the back. Postural exercises such as Pilates or yoga can help restore the core muscles and helps with breathing.

On the onset of a dyspepsia attack, I find this particular stretch helpful:

1. Lift your arms up directly in front of you at 90 degrees.
2. Take a deep breath and in a semi-circular motion lift them up over your head while stretching them out, keeping your back straight.
3. Then bring them back down while stretching them out at the same time and breathing out. You could hold on to the top of a doorway and keep your arms up for 10 seconds before you bring them back down again, Repeat 5 times.
4. Afterwards, sit down, keep your back straight so you don't put pressure on your stomach. Drink a little warm water. Avoid rich or oily food for the rest of the day.

Acupuncture & Osteopathy

I have more recently discovered the healing powers of acupuncture and it's opened up a whole new world of Chinese medicine which I didn't really know about before. Thanks to Mandeep Nandhra, a brilliant Acupuncturist and Osteopath, I now know a lot more about the role of the spleen.

This new knowledge has reaffirmed to me that my digestive woes at least partly stem from excessive emotional worry, which was initially triggered when my first daughter was born. I've noticed it repeatedly happen during times of emotional upset such as illnesses in the family or when hearing about sad news affecting people I care about.

I have learned from Mandeep that, in the world of acupuncture, your spleen governs digestion. It is responsible for converting the food that we eat into Qi (energy) that drives the body. Indeed, she identified that my spleen was a little weakened (she could tell this by looking at my tongue).

In Chinese Medicine, our organs are affected by emotions. The spleen is affected by the emotion of worry. So overthinking, as you would with stress and anxiety, will weaken the spleen.

"Weakened spleen Qi can make the digestive system sluggish, which will have an impact on digestion and can lead to bloating, abdominal distension / discomfort, feeling tired, a heavy sensation in the body and feeling cold. Acupuncture can help by restoring balance to the organs."

MANDEEP NANDHRA, ACUPUNCTURIST AND OSTEOPATH, INNATE VITALITY

Mandeep explained to me that the spleen is further influenced by the intake of cold raw food, greasy food, overly spicy food and not eating at regular times. It is also affected by exposure to a cold and damp environment.

Acupuncture can help by restoring balance to the organs, which is done by choosing the appropriate acupuncture points. Sometimes other modalities like moxibustion, Guasha sha and cupping are used in conjunction with needles to encourage warmth and strengthen Qi, as well as to move stagnation and allow the Qi to move freely. In simple terms, stagnation causes discomfort and pain. Acupuncture also has an overall effect on the body and encourages it to move towards relaxation and calm, putting it into a parasympathetic state.

"Osteopathy can also be utilised to treat digestive issues by promoting lymphatic movement, as well as freeing restrictions in the body at sites that correspond to the digestive system", adds Mandeep.

As most health practitioners will agree, Mandeep advises not to withdraw PPI medications suddenly. Always discuss your options to wean off them and explore other treatments with your GP. She says simple changes to your diet and lifestyle can have a big impact on digestive issues – something I can certainly testify to.

Since this is a guide for foodies, the next section is all about food. Please stay optimistic that you will be able to enjoy a variety of food again even if you can't tolerate them all right now.

Foods to add, avoid and reduce

During dyspepsia flare-ups I find it helpful to stick to bland foods like boiled egg on toast or chicken slices sans seasoning. Sometimes I eliminate bread altogether for a while as it can be heavy on the stomach. This gives your gut a chance to heal itself.

Alcohol is a big trigger for me even nowadays so I can't get away with drinking more than a glass of wine at the best of times. Fizzy drinks are another thing to avoid. A few sips here and there seem to be ok.

But remember, everyone has different food triggers. Whilst you may be able to tolerate some foods in moderation, other people may not tolerate those at all without it causing them pain, and vice versa.

Hopefully in time, once your gut has healed, you will be able to have all the foods you love again, even if only in moderation. I was certainly overjoyed when I could have things like chocolate and muffins again. But I have to take care not to binge on them.

If you're suffering from dyspepsia, you might find the lists below handy as a guide of food choices to increase, avoid or reduce. It's not an exhaustive list and you may want to make your own to stick on your fridge.

Add

- Bone broth
- Liquorice
- Steamed food
- Lemons
- Potatoes and sweet potatoes
- Manuka honey
- Asparagus
- Mustard
- Salmon
- Camomile tea
- Red bush tea
- Egg
- Yoghurt
- Cabbage
- Celery
- Turmeric
- Avocado
- Probiotics
- Fenugreek seeds
- Ricotta cheese
- Coconut milk
- Almond milk
- Kombucha
- Apple cider vinegar
- Olives

Avoid

- Alcohol
- Fizzy drinks
- Very spicy food
- Oily or fried food
- NSAIDs
- Over-eating (stop eating before you're completely full, chew food well and eat slowly).

Reduce

- Medicines
- Pastries
- Bread
- Chocolate
- Biscuits
- Pasteurised dairy e.g. cheese
- Grilled or baked food
- Gluten

The benefits of steam cooking

As healthy cooking has become a big thing in our household, it's been fascinating to learn about the benefits of steaming food. Even nowadays, fried and greasy foods, especially chorizo sausage, can cause me excruciating stomach pain.

I tend to use a bamboo steamer for dim sum and veggies, and a stainless steel one for meat, lentils and poultry. I quite often steam veggies for my baby daughter too. In fact, it's great for the whole family, not to mention good fun!

Steaming food is a healthy and economical way of cooking:
1. It's good for your heart: No need to add fats or oils.
2. It retains more original vitamins, minerals and enzymes.
3. It softens the fibres of vegetables and fruits, making them more easily digestible, so your body can absorb all that nutritional goodness more easily.
4. It retains the original structure and colours of the foods.
5. You can cook a variety of foods quickly over one heat supply.

Sample dyspepsia meal plan

Try to include a variety of gut-friendly ingredients in your meals throughout the week, rather than overeating one particular food type. Below is just an example to inspire your meal-planning, including some economical use of leftovers.

MONDAY

BREAKFAST: PORRIDGE WITH OAT MILK /COCONUT MILK, CINNAMON AND HONEY

LUNCH: POACHED EGG ON SOURDOUGH BREAD WITH AVOCADO

DINNER: CABBAGE & LAMB STEW

DESSERT: BLUEBERRY MUFFINS

TUESDAY

BREAKFAST: BRAN FLAKES WITH ALMOND MILK

LUNCH: COOKED CHICKEN SLICES, HUMMUS AND VEGETABLE CRUDITÉS

DINNER: SALMON WITH STEAMED CUMIN CAULIFLOWER

DESSERT: KEFIR YOGHURT WITH MANUKA HONEY

WEDNESDAY

BREAKFAST: MUESLI WITH COCONUT MILK / ALMOND MILK

LUNCH: SMOKED SALMON AND RICOTTA CHEESE ON SOURDOUGH TOAST

DINNER: CABBAGE & LAMB STEW (LEFTOVERS FROM MONDAY)

DESSERT: YOGHURT ICE-CREAM WITH BLUEBERRIES

THURSDAY

BREAKFAST: PORRIDGE WITH HONEY AND CASHEW NUTS

LUNCH: AVOCADO & OLIVE BRUSCHETTA

DINNER: SOOTHING CHICKEN & VEGETABLE BROTH

DESSERT: STEAMED CINNAMON PEACHES

FRIDAY

BREAKFAST: OATS PRE-SOAKED IN ALMOND MILK IN THE FRIDGE OVERNIGHT. SPRINKLE WALNUTS AND DRIZZLE HONEY ON TOP WHEN READY TO EAT

LUNCH: BONE BROTH OR LEFTOVERS FROM THURSDAY'S DINNER

DINNER: BAKED AUBERGINE AND STEAMED ASPARAGUS SIDE

DESSERT: KEFIR YOGHURT WITH MANUKA HONEY AND BLUEBERRIES

SATURDAY

BREAKFAST: POACHED EGG ON SOURDOUGH TOAST WITH AVOCADO

LUNCH: BONE BROTH

DINNER: LENTIL SOUP

DESSERT: STEAMED NECTARINES WITH YOGURT ICE-CREAM

SUNDAY

BREAKFAST: PORRIDGE

LUNCH: AVOCADO & OLIVE BRUSCHETTA

DINNER: STEAMED CHICKEN, CARROT & COURGETTE

DESSERT: GREEK YOGHURT WITH A SQUEEZE OF HONEY

Gut-friendly
RECIPES

You might look at some of those recipes and think, err that's not dyspepsia-friendly! Let's be realistic, we don't want to eat bland soup forever, so whilst some are very dyspepsia-friendly for those days you're really struggling (think steam cooking), most of them are flexible gut-friendly recipes to help you maintain a healthy digestive system.

Feel free to substitute ingredients according to your needs. From starters and light bites to marvellous mains and scrumptious desserts, some are my own creations and some have been kindly contributed by others.

All are intended to be nutritious and delicious.

Scrumptious STARTERS & LIGHT BITES

SCRUMPTIOUS STARTERS & LIGHT BITES

Lemony Steamed Asparagus

Asparagus stabilises digestion due to the high amount of fibre and protein that it contains, which help move food through the gut and provide relief and discomfort. It is also high in anti-inflammatory nutrients and provides a wide variety of antioxidant nutrients, including vitamin C, beta-carotene, vitamin E, and the minerals zinc, manganese and selenium. Steaming asparagus, rather than frying or boiling, helps retain more nutrients.

Serves 4 | Takes 15 minutes

Ingredients:

- 400g asparagus tips
- 2 tbsp lemon juice
- 2 tsp extra virgin olive oil
- 1 tsp turmeric

Method:

1. Place the asparagus in a steamer, cover with the lid and steam for 10 minutes.
2. Mix the olive oil, turmeric and lemon juice together.
3. Place the asparagus in a bowl, pour over the lemony oil, combine well, season and serve.

SCRUMPTIOUS STARTERS & LIGHT BITES

Steamed Aromatic Cumin Cauliflower

Cauliflower is a good source of fibre for feeding the healthy bacteria in your gut that help reduce inflammation and promote digestive health. Why not throw in some broccoli too!

Serves 4 | Takes 20 minutes

Ingredients

- 600g cauliflower florets (or substitute some with broccoli)
- 2 tsp ground cumin
- 2 tsp turmeric
- 4 tbsp Greek yoghurt
- 4 tsp lemon juice
- Salt & pepper to taste

Method:

1. Combine the cauliflower, cumin, turmeric and a pinch of salt together. You can omit the salt for babies / toddlers.
2. Place the spiced florets into the steamer. Cover with the lid and steam for 15 minutes or until tender. Remove and leave to cool for one minute so the steam doesn't split the yoghurt dressing.
3. Mix together the yoghurt and lemon juice in a bowl. Add the cauliflower florets. Combine well, season and serve.

SCRUMPTIOUS STARTERS & LIGHT BITES

Avocado & Olive Bruschetta

Avocado is a superfood packed with fibre and essential nutrients, such as potassium, which helps promote healthy digestive function. If tomatoes or onions trigger your dyspepsia then simply leave them out this time.

Makes 8 | Takes 20 minutes

Ingredients:

- 2 baguettes
- Extra virgin olive oil
- 4 vine tomatoes
- 1 ripe avocado

- 2 heaped tbsp black olives
- 1 onion (optional)
- 4 slices serrano ham
- 8 dollops kefir / Greek yoghurt

Method:

1. Preheat the oven to 200C. Halve each baguette lengthways then cut each in half. Place on a baking tray, drizzle bread with olive oil, top with wedges of tomato and onion, and another drizzle of olive oil. Place in the oven for 4 minutes.
2. Meanwhile, stone, peel and slice the avocado.
3. Remove the bruschetta from the oven and pile on the avocado, olives and ham then return to the oven for 5 minutes until crisp and golden.
4. Top with dollops of yoghurt and tuck in.

SCRUMPTIOUS STARTERS & LIGHT BITES

Mentally Good Lentil Soup

Lentils are high in fibre, which supports regular bowel movements and the growth of healthy gut bacteria. Leave out the onions, carrots, leeks and chopped tomatoes if you wish. Add a spoon of yoghurt to add probiotic goodness and a creamy texture.

Serves 4 | Takes 1 hour

Ingredients:

- 2 litres stock
- A knob of butter
- 150g red lentils, rinsed
- Vegetables, finely chopped e.g. carrots / leeks/potatoes
- 400g chopped tomatoes

- 1 clove garlic chopped
- 1 onion chopped (optional)
- 1 tbsp turmeric; 1 tbsp cumin
- Salt and pepper to season
- Parsley to serve

Method:

1. Fry the onion and garlic in butter in a large saucepan. Add turmeric and cumin. Pour in stock and add lentils. Bring to the boil and allow the lentils to soften for 3-5 minutes.
2. Add the carrots and leeks then season with salt and pepper to taste. Reduce the heat, stir in the chopped tomatoes, cover and simmer for 45 minutes or until the lentils have fully turned to mush.
3. Scatter over the parsley and serve.

SCRUMPTIOUS STARTERS & LIGHT BITES
Poached Egg on Sourdough with Avocado

Eggs are easier to digest than some other high-protein foods. Make sure the eggs are really fresh as they will have a thicker white near the yolk that will better hold a round shape as they cook.

Serves 2 | Takes 15 minutes

Ingredients:

- 4 slices sourdough bread
- 1 large ripe avocado, destoned, peeled and mashed
- 2 fresh eggs, washed
- 1 tbsp apple cider vinegar
- Smoked salmon (optional)

Method:

1. Crack each egg into a separate cup. Bring a saucepan of water (at least 5cm deep) to a simmer and add a tbsp of apple cider vinegar. Make a swirl in the water with a spoon and slide one egg into the swirl. Repeat for the second egg. Cook for 3-4 minutes or until the egg white is set.
2. Meanwhile, toast the bread and spread with mashed avocado. Top with smoked salmon.
3. Lift each egg out with a slotted spoon and drain it on kitchen paper. Then place each one on the pre-prepared toast and serve.

SCRUMPTIOUS STARTERS & LIGHT BITES
Baked Aubergine with Yoghurt Dressing

Can be eaten hot or cold. To make it a main meal, serve with a side of quinoa or rice, salad and hummus. Or chips (you didn't hear that from me).

Serves 4 | Takes 1 hour

Ingredients:

- 2 aubergines
- 5 tbsp extra virgin olive oil
- 1 sprinkle sea salt flakes; 1 tsp black pepper; 1 tsp ground cumin or turmeric
- 200g kefir / Greek yoghurt

- 1 clove garlic, finely crushed
- 3 tbsp lemon juice
- 2 tbsp pumpkin seeds; 1 handful basil leaves / dried basil

Method:

1. Preheat oven to 200C. Cut each aubergine in half lengthways. Score the flesh of each half with deep diagonal criss-cross cuts. Brush the surface of each half with olive oil until it fills the cuts. Sprinkle with salt, pepper and cumin. Roast for 40 minutes until soft and brown.
2. Dressing: In a bowl, whisk the yoghurt, crushed garlic, lemon juice and 3 tbsp olive oil until smooth. Season to taste and leave to chill.
3. To serve, drizzle the yoghurt sauce over the aubergine, sprinkle on the seeds and season to taste.

SCRUMPTIOUS STARTERS & LIGHT BITES

Cooling Tappouli

Tappouli AKA tabbouleh / tabbouli is one of my family favourites and super healthy. Mint, onions and tomatoes could be dyspepsia triggers so if they are then it might be best to hold off until you can eat them.

Serves 4-6 | Takes a long time (1.5 hours approx)

Ingredients:

- 200g (7 oz) bulgur wheat
- Salt
- ½ cucumber seeded and finely chopped
- 2 medium tomatoes, skinned, de-seeded and cut into tiny cubes
- 3 tbsp spring onions

- 3 tbsp finely chopped mint
- 200g finely chopped washed fresh parsley (must be dry to chop very finely)
- 4 tbsp lemon juice (to taste)
- 4-6 tbsp extra virgin olive oil
- To serve: 1 bunch cos lettuce and pitta bread (optional)

Method:

1. Put the bulgur wheat in a bowl, add 2 tsp salt and cover with hot water. Leave to soak for 30 minutes.
2. Put the bulgur wheat into a mixing bowl and stir in all the other ingredients. Serve in small bowls on its own or with pitta bread or lettuce, or as a side salad with your main meal.

Marvellous
MAINS

MARVELLOUS MAINS

Soothing Chicken & Vegetable Broth

This is so versatile, you can add/omit ingredients as you like. Chicken broth is an ancient remedy for fighting inflammation and healing your gut. This is one variation I created and I like to add extra lemon juice for taste and a vitamin C boost. Do include garlic and onion unless you really can't tolerate them.

Serves 4 | Takes 1.5 hours

Ingredients:

- Juice of 1 lemon
- 4 chicken drumsticks / wings
- 4 cloves garlic, halved
- 1 onion, quartered
- 4 celery sticks, washed and chopped into 1 cm pieces.

- 2 carrots, peeled, washed and chopped into 1 cm pieces.
- 2 white potatoes, peeled and quartered
- 1 tbsp turmeric; 1 tsp cumin; 1 tsp cinnamon; black pepper

Method:

1. Place the chicken in a large pot and cover with cold water, bring to the boil and simmer for 30 minutes. With a large spoon, skim off and discard the scum that rises to the top. Top up with more water if needed.
2. Throw in the vegetables, onion, spices, garlic and lemon. Season to taste. Simmer for 40 minutes. Remove the bones if you wish. Serve on its own or on a bed of rice, with or without bread. Breathe in the steam while it's still hot and sip the warm broth.

MARVELLOUS MAINS

Steamed Chicken, Carrot & Courgette

This dish includes a variety of vegetables along with protein-rich chicken. Skip the onion and garlic if you can't tolerate them. Make the meal go further with couscous, quinoa or rice.

Serves 4 | Takes 45 minutes

Ingredients:

- 4 chicken breasts
- 2 garlic cloves, crushed
- 2 tsp olive oil
- 2 courgettes, thinly sliced lengthways

- 1 carrot, peeled into ribbons
- ½ onion, finely chopped
- 150g spinach
- 2 tsp freshly squeezed lemon juice

Method:

1. Place the chicken in a stainless steel steamer. Mix the garlic and olive oil and brush over the chicken. Lay the courgette slices, carrot ribbons and chopped onions on top of the chicken.
2. Cover and steam for 20 minutes or until the chicken is cooked through.
3. Put the spinach into a colander and pour boiling water over it to wilt the spinach. Transfer the spinach to a bowl and toss with the lemon juice.
4. Remove the chicken and vegetable parcel from the steamer. Slice the chicken into strips. Serve in a large serving dish with the vegetables and add the spinach on top. Drizzle with olive oil, pour the lemon juice over and serve.

MARVELLOUS MAINS

Moroccan Spiced Sweet Potato & Bone Broth Stew

Thank you to Linda Booth from Just for Tummies for this gut-healing recipe.

Serves 4 | Takes 1 hour approx.

Ingredients:

- 4 tomatoes, halved
- 5 tbsp olive oil or ghee
- 250g sweet potato, peeled and chopped into large chunks
- 1 tbsp thyme or ½ tbsp dried
- 1 garlic clove, crushed
- 2 x 400g cans chickpeas
- 200g cavolo nero, shredded

- 1 tbsp ground cumin; 1 tsp turmeric; 1 tsp ground coriander
- 1 bay leaf
- 1 tbsp harissa
- ½ cup raisins
- 1 litre bone broth / veg stock
- Fresh coriander leaves

Method:

1. Heat oven to 200C/180C fan. Put the tomatoes on a baking sheet lined with baking parchment, drizzle over 2 tbsp olive oil, season and roast in the oven for 20 mins or until soft. Set aside.
2. Meanwhile, pour 2 tbsp olive oil into a large saucepan and add the squash, thyme and garlic. Season generously and cook on low heat for 15 mins or until the vegetables begin to soften.
3. Add the tomatoes, drained chickpeas, cavolo nero, bay leaf, ground spices, raisins and harissa. Season to taste and pour in the broth or stock. Bring to the boil, then reduce the heat and simmer for 30-35 mins until the liquid has reduced.
4. Serve the stew in bowls and top with a sprinkling of coriander leaves. Serve either on its own or with fluffy quinoa.

MARVELLOUS MAINS

Cabbage & Lamb Stew

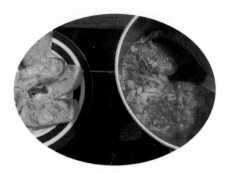

Cabbage is good for your digestive system as it contains nutrients that protect your stomach lining and intestines. Its juice can also help stomach ulcers to heal. You can use a jar of sauerkraut instead of fresh cabbage if you prefer. My family loves this dish with garlic bread on the side.

Serves 4 | Takes 1 hour

Ingredients:

- 2 tbsp olive oil
- 2 carrots, diced
- 2 celery sticks, diced
- 4 garlic cloves, chopped
- 1 head green cabbage, halved, cored, cut into 1-inch cubes
- 1.5 lbs stewing lamb, cubed
- 1 litre cups chicken broth / stock
- 1.5 tsp salt
- ½ tsp black pepper
- 1.5 tbsp apple cider vinegar
- 2 tsp dried thyme
- ½ tsp caraway seeds (optional)
- 2 bay leaves (optional)
- ¼ tsp cayenne pepper
- 1 can white beans, drained
- Fresh parsley
- Grated parmesan cheese

Method:

1. Heat the oil in a sauté pan and add the rinsed carrots, celery and garlic. Sauté for 5 mins.
2. Add the cabbage, lamb, broth, salt, pepper, vinegar, thyme, caraway, cayenne and bay leaves. Stir. Cover and simmer for 40 minutes.
3. Add canned white beans and heat through. Serve in bowls with parsley and crusty bread.

MARVELLOUS MAINS

Pretty in Pink Salmon 'n' Slaw

An acupuncturist can tell by looking at your tongue if you have a blood deficiency which may not be picked up in regular blood tests. It turns out beetroot is hugely beneficial as well as delicious so I try and include it in my diet as with this recipe.

Serves 2 | Takes 20 minutes

Ingredients:

- 200g beetroot slaw
- 70g feta cheese, chopped into small cubes
- 2 skin-on boneless salmon fillets
- 200g quinoa (or couscous / rice if preferred)
- 2 limes, cut into wedges
- Beetroot hummus (optional)
- Kefir or Greek yoghurt (optional)

Method:

1. Start cooking the quinoa, couscous or rice according to the packet instructions.
2. Season the salmon. Heat 2 tbsp olive oil on high heat in a non-stick frying pan. Add the salmon skin side down and heat for 3 minutes. Flip over and heat for another 4-5 minutes. Alternatively you could steam or poach the salmon.
3. Serve with the beetroot slaw and feta along with quinoa/rice/couscous and lime wedges.
4. Add a few dollops of yoghurt and / or beetroot hummus on the side if you wish.

MARVELLOUS MAINS

Homely Dolma

Thank you to my mum for reciting her Iraqi dolma recipe over the phone to me during the Covid-19 pandemic lockdown in April 2020. I've always wanted to learn how to cook it and finally had a spare weekend. Serve with pitta bread and a yoghurt / hummus dip. Goes well with tappouli salad too as part of a mezze.

Serves 4 | Takes a long time. 2.5 hours approx.

Ingredients:

- **Half** mug mince lamb
- 1 mug rice (soaked for 1 hour)
- 2 bunches Swiss chard / vine leaves (destemmed)
- Carrots (peeled and halved)
- 1 tbsp margarine

- 1 tsp spices (any you like)
- Pinch of salt and black pepper
- 4 tsp pomegranate molasses
- 4 garlic cloves, crushed
- 3 tbsp tomato puree
- Olive oil

Method:

1. Mix the mince and rice with garlic, spices, 3 tsp pomegranate molasses, salt, 2 tbsp tomato purée and 1 tbsp margarine. Make into a patty.
2. Par boil water in saucepan and place 2-3 leaves at a time to soften them for 3 minutes approx and set aside. Stuff 1 tbsp of the meat mixture into each leaf and roll. Put in the freezer for 1 hour to set.
3. To cook the dolmas: Heat 2 tbsp olive oil in a saucepan, arrange the sliced carrots at the bottom and dolmas on top. Mix ½ mug cold water with 1 tbsp tomato purée and 1 tbsp pomegranate molasses and stir. Pour it over the top of the dolmas. It should only cover the base or half way. Cover the dolmas with a non-plastic lid e.g. a thick plate or metal saucepan lid to keep them pressed down and then cover the whole saucepan with its own lid. Cook for half an hour and serve.

MARVELLOUS MAINS

Mama's Veggie Biryani

Thank you to my mum for this recipe over the phone as well. This is one of her specialties with my own twist. I like to serve it with grilled halloumi and baked potatoes chopped into small cubes. You can add chicken to make it a chicken and vegetable biryani. You can also add coriander, cumin, cinnamon, roasted cashews and ginger.

Serves 4 | Takes 45 minutes

Ingredients:

- 2 tbsp olive oil
- Chopped onions (1-3 onions depending on how much you like onions)
- 1 tsp turmeric; 1 tbsp curry powder; ½ tsp biryani spices or chilli powder

- ½ freshly squeezed lemon
- Mixed veg (frozen/fresh)
- 2 mugs rice; 2 mugs water
- 4 white potatoes, cubed, boiled then oven baked
- Hard-boiled egg (optional)

Method:

1. Fry the chopped onions in the oil with turmeric, curry powder and chilli powder/biryani spices. Add the lemon juice, mixed veg and season. Add the rice and water. Bring to the boil, turn down the heat and simmer for 25 minutes, covered.
2. Boil and bake the diced potatoes. Hard-boil an egg if using.
3. Serve in bowls with potatoes and sliced egg over the top, and pitta bread on the side.

MARVELLOUS MAINS

Bone Broth Bolognese

Thank you to Rachel Down, Founder of Boil & Broth, for this recipe. Rachel says: "You can serve it with pasta, although pasta contains gluten so if you are gluten conscious, then serve this with quinoa and salad. It's delicious."

Serves 4 | Takes 50 minutes

Ingredients:

- 1 tbsp olive oil
- 500g turkey mince
- 150g smoked bacon cut in small pieces
- 400ml beef broth
- 1/2 broccoli chopped

- 1 red pepper chopped
- 2 small brown onions chopped
- 100g tomato puree
- 1/2 tsp cayenne pepper
- 1 tbsp smoked paprika; 1 tsp pepper

Method:

1. In a wok, heat the oil then add the turkey mince and bacon. Cook for 5-minutes. Add broccoli, red pepper and onions to the wok, stir and continue to cook on medium further 3-minutes.
2. Add the bone broth and tomato puree. Stir together. Cover and let it simmer for 20-minutes, checking and stirring occasionally.
3. Add the cayenne, paprika and pepper. Stir together and cook for a further 2-minutes. Serve with quinoa and spinach.

Delectable
DESSERTS

DELECTABLE DESSERTS

Warm Blueberry & Coconut Muffins

Another gem of a recipe from the lovely Rachel Down, Founder of Boil & Broth. These muffins use coconut sugar as a healthy alternative to regular sugar. They also include fresh detoxing blueberries. It's healthy, so easy to make (a bonus as I'm no pro baker) and most importantly, delicious. I like to drink red bush tea with it for a warming and refreshing accompaniment.

Makes 12 muffins | Takes 40 minutes

Ingredients:

- 150g butter
- 150g coconut sugar
- 3 beaten eggs
- 150g plain flour

- 1 tsp baking powder
- 75g blueberries
- 50g coconut shredding

Method:

1. Preheat oven to 170C. In a pot, melt the butter on low then take off the heat. Pour the butter into a mixing bowl and mix in the coconut sugar. Add the flour, baking powder and beaten eggs and keep stirring. Add the coconut and blueberries.
2. Spoon the cake mixture into muffin cases in equal amounts. Bake in the oven for 20 minutes.

DELECTABLE DESSERTS

Kefir Yoghurt with Manuka Honey

Kefir is a probiotic made by fermenting milk. It is an even more potent source of probiotics than plain yoghurt. It can improve reflux symptoms by feeding the good bacteria in your gut. Manuka honey's anti-inflammatory and antiseptic properties help reduce the pain caused by dyspepsia. Its antioxidant properties help remove free radicals that may damage the digestive tract.

Serves 4 | Takes 5 minutes tops

Ingredients:

- 350g tub kefir natural yoghurt
- 4 tbsp manuka honey

Method:

1. Divide up the yoghurt between 4 bowls.
2. Drizzle 1 tbsp of manuka honey on top of each dish.
3. Enjoy.

DELECTABLE DESSERTS

Cinnamon Peaches

You could substitute peaches with another fruit such as nectarines or apples. You could also use tinned peaches to save time but you probably won't get the same health benefits as steaming.

Serves 2 | Takes 35 minutes

Ingredients:

- 2 fresh peaches
- 2 tsp freshly grated ginger
- 1 tsp cinnamon
- 1 tbsp coconut sugar
- 2 tbsp yoghurt / yoghurt ice-cream

Method:

1. Cut the peaches in half and remove the stone.
2. Distribute the chopped ginger evenly over the upturned peach halves and sprinkle with the coconut sugar and cinnamon.
3. Place the peaches in a steamer and steam for 20 minutes.
4. Serve with a few dollops of yoghurt or yoghurt ice cream.

DELECTABLE DESSERTS

Rose Water Beetroot Brownies

You might have to wait until your dyspepsia is under control before you start eating brownies again but this is a relatively healthy version. Use 100g cooking chocolate and 50g butter instead to make chocolate brownies without beetroot.

Makes 12 | Takes 50 minutes

Ingredients:

- 150g raw beetroot (use gloves)
- 2 eggs
- 150g runny honey
- 1 tbsp rose water
- 100g self-raising flour or gluten-free flour
- 50g cocoa powder
- Pinch of salt
- 1 tsp baking powder
- Icing sugar for dusting

Method:

1. Boil the beetroot on the hob until tender. Once cooled, peel and grate it.
2. Grease a baking tray (20x25cm approx) and line the base with parchment paper. Preheat the oven to 170C.
3. Mix eggs, honey and salt in a bowl for 5 minutes. Add the dry ingredients and mix.
4. Add the beetroot to the bowl. Add the rose water. Mix well and pour into the baking tray. Smooth the top with a spatula.
5. Bake for 30 minutes. Cool and cut. Dust with a little icing sugar.

Delicious DRINKS

DELICIOUS DRINKS

I sometimes find a simple cup of hot water helps ease mild indigestion. However, there are many other drinks that are claimed to be beneficial for your digestive system and can help prevent and soothe dyspepsia. Here are a few that I've found helpful but bear in mind these might not all be suitable for everyone so if in doubt speak to your doctor, a nutritionist or do some online research of your own to find out any possible side effects.

Bone broths

If your oesophagus has been damaged by acid reflux, bone broth could help restore its lining. Bone broth is rich in gelatin and cartilage, which are essential for rebuilding tissue. It also carries amino acids, minerals, electrolytes and antioxidants that help heal the gastrointestinal tract. Beef bone broth is the most natural source of collagen.

Honey and lemon water

Add a squeeze of honey and half a fresh lemon into a cup of warm water. Ideally drink it when you first wake up as it will help to kick-start your digestive system, allowing you to digest food more easily and help prevent the build-up of toxins. For an even bigger health boost you could add cinnamon, turmeric or ginger. You could freeze the lemon juice in ice cubes ready to drop in to your water as needed.

Rose water

Rose water can help with bloating and upset stomach by increasing bile flow. It can also work as a laxative effect by increasing the amount of water in the faeces and the frequency of going to the toilet. Inhaling its fumes can also help you relax and lift your mood. Add a drop to a glass of water or for extra throat comfort use warm water to make a simple homemade rose water tea. You can also get rose tea leaves to brew a proper cuppa.

Kombucha

A fermented, lightly effervescent, sweetened black or green tea drink rich in probiotics. Be aware it contains small amounts of caffeine and alcohol (eight bottles is equivalent to a beer) and is unpasteurised. Drinking too much of it can lead to excess sugar and calorie intake and side effects like digestive distress.

Turmeric latte

Turmeric aids digestion with its antioxidant and anti-inflammatory properties. Add a pinch of black pepper to enhance absorption of its bioactive compound curcumin.

Celery juice

Very alkalising, detoxifying and nutritious, packed with multivitamins.

Camomile tea

Camomile has a reputation for calming digestive issues. Drink one cup of camomile tea about 45 minutes before bed.

Kefir water

Dairy-free and vegan-friendly, this tasty beverage offers beneficial bacteria and yeast and has been shown to boost immunity and slow cancer cell growth. Start by drinking small quantities in case it causes any side effects. You may want to check with your doctor before drinking this if you have a condition that weakens your immune system as concerns have been raised about probiotic use in people with immune function.

Tummy tea

Hand-blended in Kent, Tummy Tea from Just for Tummies is a calming, healthy, herbal tea with a blend of herbs and spices including liquorice root and fenugreek seed, traditionally used to soothe the digestive system.

Green tea

Promotes overall digestion by breaking down food, as well as refreshing, rehydrating and cleansing your system. It contains catechins that help to soothe muscles in the gastrointestinal tract.

Peppermint tea

It has an antispasmodic effect on the body which can help relieve stomach problems like nausea and indigestion. However, mint can trigger acid reflux for some people as it relaxes the sphincter muscle between the stomach and oesophagus, which allows stomach acids to flow back into the oesophagus. Try it and see if it helps or hinders you.

Red bush tea

One of my all-time favourites, red bush (aka rooibos) is naturally caffeine-free and contains several compounds that may help relax the digestive system and relieve discomfort.

Checklist to avoid dyspepsia

A combination of the following may work for you. They usually work for me. Check with your doctor or suitable therapist if you're unsure.

1. Chew food well.
2. Don't overeat (if possible, make your last meal of the day the smallest one).
3. Take a break from trigger foods and reintroduce them slowly.
4. Breathe deeply, in through your nose and out through your mouth.
5. Manage your anxiety.
6. Eat foods that heal your gut.
7. Relax when you eat.
8. Try to stay sitting down for a while after eating, and avoid bending to stack the dishwasher straight away.
9. Have a warm drink after a meal.
10. Avoid drinking water during your meal. Instead, drink water half an hour before and after.
11. Take a good probiotic supplement like Just for Tummies' Live Bacteria or Holland & Barrett Acidophilus (check with your doctor or a nutritionist first if you have a compromised immune system or take any other medication).
12. Dilute 1 tbsp apple cider vinegar in a small glass of water and drink before lunch and dinner every day for two weeks.

Acknowledgements

Thank you to the following people for contributing their expertise to this guide:

Linda Booth, Naturopath and Founder, Just for Tummies
In her 28+ years in the field of natural medicine, Linda has built a large network of healthcare professionals, both from orthodox and complementary medicine, enabling her to assess a person's symptoms and refer them to the right practitioner for the treatment that she feels will help them. She is a results-driven therapist with a holistic and wholistic approach to her practice, using a combination of her targeted supplements and dietary/lifestyle advice to bring remarkable results to the many thousands of people she has treated.

Get 20% off your first order on https://justfortummies.co.uk

Rachel Down, Founder, Boil & Broth
Rachel Down is Founder of Boil and Broth. She is a mum, a wife and also studying a Health Science degree. Rachel is passionate about encouraging people to take control of their health; spiritually, physically and emotionally. She believes in diet before drugs and natural medicine.

Get 10% off orders on https://www.boilandbroth.com. Use offer code LOVEYOURGUT

Albert Dutoit, Advanced Clinical and Sports Massage Therapist
Albert is registered with the Complimentary and Natural Healthcare Council. He is a member of the Professional Association of Clinical Therapists and the Federation of Holistic Therapists.

Visit: https://albertdutoit.com

Mandeep Nandhra, Acupuncturist and Osteopath
Mandeep is registered with the General Osteopathic Council and the Association of Traditional Chinese Medicine. She helps people lead healthier, more energetic lives by providing non-invasive and non-surgical wellness treatment.

Visit: https://innatevitality.co.uk

Printed in Great Britain
by Amazon

55714776R00030